BORN TO RACE

First published in 2026 by OH
An Imprint of HEADLINE PUBLISHING GROUP LIMITED

1

Disclaimer:
This book has not been licensed, approved, sponsored, or endorsed by Oscar Piastri

Oscar Piastri is a registered trademark owned by Rising Sun 81 Limited, La Tonnelle House, Les Banques, St Sampson, GY1 3HS, Guernsey

Cataloguing in Publication Data is available from the British Library

ISBN 978-1-03544-003-0

Compiled and written by David Clayton
Editorial: Matt Tomlinson
Designed and typeset in Queulat by Stephen Cary
Project manager: Russell Porter
Illustration by Ryan Adley
Production: Marion Storz
Printed and bound in Dubai

Headline's policy is to use papers that are natural, renewable and recyclable products and made from wood grown in well-managed forests and other controlled sources. The logging and manufacturing processes are expected to conform to the environmental regulations of the country of origin.

HEADLINE PUBLISHING GROUP LIMITED
An Hachette UK Company
Carmelite House, 50 Victoria Embankment, London EC4Y 0DZ

The authorised representative in the EEA is Hachette Ireland, 8 Castlecourt Centre, Dublin 15, D15 XTP3, Ireland (email: info@hbgi.ie)

www.headline.co.uk www.hachette.co.uk

BORN TO RACE

THE LITTLE GUIDE TO

OSCAR PIASTRI

UNOFFICIAL AND UNAUTHORIZED

CONTENTS

INTRODUCTION

Oscar Piastri's star is on the rise – and at a meteoric rate.

By 2025, the 24-year-old was vying to become the third Australian to take the Formula 1 crown as he went head-to-head with British McLaren teammate Lando Norris.

It could be a rivalry that lasts for many years, and one that is already capturing the imagination of race fans around the globe.

McLaren has a rich history of incredible drivers, and Piastri already looks set to join the other legends. But will Piastri and Norris replicate the fierce competition of Lewis Hamilton and Max Verstappen, or even reach the notorious dislike of Alain Prost and Ayrton Senna?

With an entire nation watching and willing his every move behind the wheel Down Under,

Piastri looks set to become a national hero, and his F1 crowning seems more a matter of when rather than if.

From his brilliance on the racetrack to his childhood in Melbourne, *The Little Guide to Oscar Piastri* provides a fascinating snapshot of a thrilling driver who could dominate for years.

Discover his influences, inspirations and aspirations in this little guide, the first collection of quotes, facts and trivia about this talented young driver.

Get to know the man behind the wheel as we track his journey so far through this carefully chosen selection of words and wisdom.

This is the ultimate companion for any fan of Piastri or Formula 1 as Piastri accelerates towards pole position.

CHAPTER ONE

Start Your Engines

From the suburban streets of Melbourne, as the Australian Grand Prix roared around Albert Park, the young Oscar Piastri was captivated – the sounds of those Formula 1 cars tipping speeds of 200mph lit a fire in the boy that would turn into an inferno. Racing was his destiny...

FACT

Oscar Jack Piastri was born on 6 April 2001 in Melbourne, Victoria, Australia.

The son of Chris and Nicole, Oscar grew up in the inner-city suburb of Brighton with his three younger sisters.

His surname comes from a mixture of Italian, Yugoslavian and Chinese heritage on his father's side, while his mother comes from Scottish and Irish stock.

"

My mum taught Oscar to play Monopoly aged four – like, way too young – then it was chess, then athletics, cricket and footy so yes, as a family, we're all super-competitive.

"

Oscar's mum (and legend), Nicole Piastri, reveals her son's early talents, The Red Flags Podcast, 2024

"

I was a competitive kid before I got into racing with all the sport that I played. Even at school, I wanted to be the smartest kid, so I think it's sort of just ingrained.

"

Oscar Piastri on his natural competitiveness, F1 Beyond the Grid podcast, March 2023

"

I first started watching F1 in around 2009 and Mark [Webber] was at Red Bull at the time and so I sort of naturally followed him because he was Australian. But when I first started watching I didn't really have anyone specific as an idol.

"

Oscar Piastri on his influences, givemesport.com, June 2023

FACT

Piastri's love of Formula 1 was influenced by living within earshot of the annual Australian Grand Prix near his home in Melbourne as cars roared by on the streets of the Albert Park Circuit.

"I always looked up to the cricketers - Ricky Ponting was kind of a hero of mine in some ways. I was lucky enough to get a photo with him many years ago, and some of the Aussie Rules football players as well."

On his sporting heroes, givemesport.com, June 2023

"We would have to read him car magazines, like, that's from the age of younger than two so before Oscar could put sentences together."

Oscar's mum, Nicole, recalling an unerring early interest in cars, thesportsrush.com, August 2024

“

I wouldn’t say I was ever good enough to make a career out of those sports, but I really enjoyed them and I think before I started racing, that’s where sort of my passion for being competitive started and then that’s sort of what translated into racing in the end.

”

Oscar on getting started, givemesport.com, June 2023

“

Before I started racing, I really enjoyed playing Aussie rules football and cricket as well, but they all kind of got swallowed up by racing when I started.

”

Oscar on his natural sporting ability, givemesport.com, June 2023

> “Oscar’s bedtime stories were mainly car books. He could recite how quick cars were, the horsepower, how much speed they had.”

Oscar’s dad, Chris Piastri, recalls his son’s early interest in motorsport,
The Sydney Morning Herald, 2021

“

I watched a lot of V8 supercars in Australia, but I didn’t really have a favourite driver or anything. I just enjoyed watching the racing.

”

Oscar on his love of all forms of racing, givemesport.com, June 2023

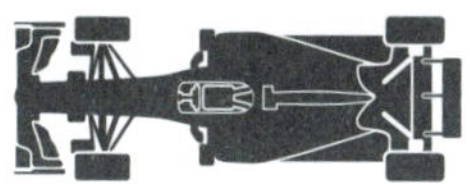

“

We bought remote-controlled cars when I was on a business trip in America and Oscar took to that incredibly. He started racing them and got third place in his first-ever event against 20- and 30-year-olds when he was just six.

”

Chris Piastri provided the spark that a young Oscar needed, The Sydney Morning Herald. 2021

“

My dad brought back a remote control car from the US to Australia, and I started just driving that around the backyard and the school oval at one point when I was six or seven, and then I started racing not long after that and it all went from there, so it’s a bit of a different entry to motorsport.

”

On his backdoor introduction to the racing world, essentiallysports.com, March 2023

FACT

Remote control cars vary in size – Oscar started with one-eighth scale and then went to a one-tenth scale.

Remote control cars look like touring cars in many ways and can go up to 110 kph top speed.

They only weigh a kilo and a half, and the operator works from a driver's stand with a radio which controls the car.

"Having raced remote control cars, I kind of had a rough idea on racing lines and how the basic principles of driving worked, so I picked it up pretty quickly. If I wasn't racing cars, then RC cars could have been a career instead."

On his youth and the possibilities of remote control driving as a living, formula3.com, October 2020

“There’s no age brackets so I was often competing against people in their twenties and thirties. I won the national championships when I was nine and I think the next youngest guy was 18, so that was nice.”

Oscar recalls his child genius days of RC driving, f1.com, 2023

"

I'm the first in my family to race myself. There's always been an interest throughout my family. My grandad and my pops were both mechanics and my dad's business is in the automotive industry. They've always had a passion for cars first and foremost, but also racing.

"

From a mechanical family if not a family of racing throroughbreds, f1.com, March 2023

"My dad was the person who introduced me to go karts and he was definitely the first influence in my career, and I would say that he is probably still the biggest as well."

Oscar on his father's early input, fiaformula2.com, April 2021

“

I loved initially the speed. I think that’s what most people love.

”

On his immediate addiction to karting, f1.com, 2023

“

The rule for my parents was you can go racing, but your grades have got to stay at the same level.

”

Sound advice from the Piastri parents, f1.com, March 2023

“

I had been to Europe before and I had been to England before, so it wasn't completely new, plus, out of all of the countries that I could have gone to, it is by far the most similar to Australia, which helped.

”

On his new life at boarding school, fiaformula2.com, July 2021

FACT

For the early part of Oscar's career, his father Chris followed his son's movements not only as his chaperone, but as his personal mechanic!

“

In Australia, there aren't really many championships, per say, it’s more like, one-off races. I only did one championship, Australian karting is a bit complicated, but I finished third in that.

”

Oscar reflects on his early karting years, elliedoesf1.com, 2020

"

When I first started [racing] it was mainly for the enjoyment. But of course there was always the end goal of being able to drive race cars for a living.

"

On his longer term ambitions, givemesport.com, June 2023

"I think if there was a turning point, it was probably when I started finishing towards the front in Australia, and I started winning a couple of races here and there and finishing in the top three of championships."

Oscar on his steady ascent in karting, givemesport.com, January 2023

"The closest track to our house was 45 minutes and Brisbane's a two hour flight away, so it's not that local, but it started to get a bit more interstate at the end."

On the difficulties of progressing in karting in Australia, f1.com, 2023

"In Australia, normally the number plates are white, but if you win a state championship you get a blue number plate. I was pretty excited to have that. That was the 'thing' to have, so that was definitely one of my biggest wins."

An early success for the budding young driver, elliedoesf1.com, 2020

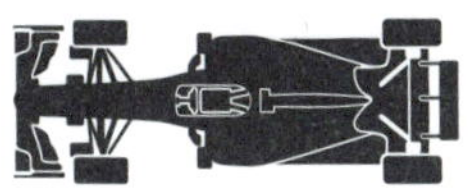

“The guy in front of me started slowing and I just thought, ‘Am I really gonna get a podium in my first international race?’”

On his dream start to life racing overseas, karting.net.au, November 2014

"I was with my dad for the first six months [in Europe] when I was 14 or 15. And then basically we got to the point where I was doing reasonably well, not amazing but good enough to keep going in Europe and we sort of had the decision of either stay in Europe and go to boarding school or go home."

On reaching a fork in the racetrack, givemesport.com, June 2023

“My kind of way of looking at that was: OK, I want to become a professional racing driver. If I can do it in Formula 1, then that's even better. And the way of getting there is by going to Europe.”

Oscar on the ultimate decision, bbc.co.uk, May 2025

"My dad wanted to go back to Australia to be with my family and just live his life as well, which is very understandable... I chose the option of staying in Europe and went to boarding school for four years, which, in hindsight, was actually a very good decision."

Oscar on his move to Europe, givemesport.com, June 2023

“I was leaving everything I knew behind, mainly just the people. I moved over with just my dad for the first six months and left my mum and three sisters at home; that wasn't easy on me but also on my dad as well.”

On the early sacrifices that he felt needed to be made, elliedoesf1.com, 2020

“

In the first six months [before boarding school], I was kind of doing online school when I could, and thinking about racing pretty much every other hour apart from that, so you can get yourself into some rabbit holes with that.

”

On life in an English school, givemesport.com, 2023

“

That started years ago when Oscar was at boarding school in the UK and he was not responding to my messages. So, I opened a Twitter account and got on there and said ‘Can you not answer?’ So that’s how it started. My plan was not to dominate the Twitter world by roasting my son.

”

Nicole Piastri explains how her life on X began by finding a communication channel her son would actually read, thesportsrush.com, August 2024

CHAPTER TWO

The Early Gears

Oscar's fledgling career was starting to take shape and the decision to relocate to Europe meant boarding school in the UK while his father returned home...

"

RFM welcomes its latest driver Oscar Piastri for OKJ in 2016... We have watched Oscar closely on the European Karting circuits and have seen him achieve some very impressive results. RFM is always looking for the next up and coming F1 drivers and it is with this in mind RFM has chosen to take Oscar on for 2016. We see him as a star of the future.

"

Oscar's new boss, Ricky Flynn, welcomes him aboard, karting.net.au, 2016

FACT

In 2016, Oscar signed with Ricky Flynn Motorsport for the 2016 European karting season.

Still only 14, the youngster would now drive the FA Kart for the highly regarded British team after feeling he'd achieved all he could in karting in Australia.

FACT

In his one and only season with Ricky Flynn Motorsport, Oscar achieved a sixth-place finish in the World Karting Championship.

"I'm really happy to finish my karting career with such a solid performance. World number 6 sounds pretty good!"

Oscar's star continues to rise, karting.net.au, November 2016

"Although Dragon F4 is a new team for this new exciting series here in the United Arab Emirates, we have handpicked our staff from top European teams to ensure that we deliver the very best support all Dragon drivers are accustomed to. Since the introduction to Oscar, we have followed his racing very carefully and look forward to welcoming this rising star to the family that is Dragon Racing."

The Dragon Racing chairman, Leon Price, on the capture of an unpolished diamond, f4uae.com, 2016

I am really happy to join Dragon Racing... We've had some really positive test days in the UK this year and I have learned a lot about the car and how to drive it, but nothing beats getting out on the track and racing wheel to wheel. I have raced at many of the world's best karting tracks over the last few years but to have my first F4 race at the Yas Marina F1 circuit is going to be pretty cool!

Oscar on his move to F4 and the opportunities that lie ahead, f4uae.com, 2016

FACT

Oscar's maiden F4 season saw him finish sixth with Dragon in the Formula 4 UAE Championship before driving for TRS Arden Junior Team (created and ran by Christian and Garry Horner) and finishing second in the 2017 F4 British Championship, winning six out of 27 races and finishing second to Britain's Jamie Caroline.

“

There was an opportunity for Red Bull to look at him at the time and we didn’t take up that option, which is something that I regret. What he went on to achieve is phenomenal, in Formula 3 and Formula 2.

”

Former Red Bull boss Christian Horner on a missed opportunity, f1.com, September 2022

“

It was good, I was sort of there or thereabouts on the pace straight away; there were a few challenges, but it was really good, I learnt a lot. Just experiencing a car racing weekend compared to karting and being on the touring car package and having fans watching for the first time, so that was cool. Just a lot of different experiences.

”

Oscar on his progression to faster cars and learning how to handle them, fiaformula4.com, 2021

“

We’ve had a strong winter test program and driving some of the most iconic tracks in the world is amazing. Having some familiar faces in the garage has allowed me to focus on learning as much as I can before the race season starts.

”

Oscar on his learning process, formulascout.com, December 2017

"We are delighted that Oscar will continue to be part of the Arden Team in 2018 and happy to be supporting him in his motorsport career."

Arden founder Garry Horner on retaining Oscar's services for the Formula Renault Eurocup in 2018, following his impressive apprenticeship at the Arden Young Driver Racing Academy, formulascout.com, December 2017

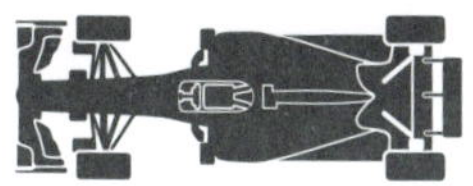

> “Arden Motorsport Formula Renault Eurocup rookie Oscar Piastri took a double podium finish at Hockenheim and two rookie wins in a brilliant weekend for the Australian driver.”

Report on ardenmotorsport.com, 2018

FACT

After a promising rookie year, the 17-year-old Oscar Piastri joined reigning champions R-ace GP for the 2019 Formula Renault Eurocup Championship in 2019.

“

I’ve had a great rookie year, learning the circuits and understanding the very high level of competition both on and off the track.

”

Oscar reflects on his year, autoaction.com, 2018

“

I’ve learned so much this year, got some decent results and I really want to take it to the next level. I think R-ace GP is a great team and I am looking forward to joining them for 2019.

”

Oscar on his next steps, autoaction.com, 2018

“

I’ve been following Oscar since mid-2017 as he was then P2 in British Formula 4 and leading the rookie standing with class. His 2018 Formula Renault campaign confirming his potential... I had the opportunity to test Oscar with the team after the final round in Barcelona and I have to say this test was more than a confirmation, it was a revelation!

”

Thibaut de Merindol, R-ace GP team principal, autoaction.com, 2018

CHAPTER THREE

Life in the Fast Lane

The teenager's rapid ascent continues with his path to Formula 1 seemingly assured – but there was still plenty of hard work ahead for the Australian...

“

Obviously that’s not the way I would have liked to win, but I’m really happy to bring R-ace GP a fifth consecutive win at Silverstone.

”

Oscar claims his first Formula Renault 2.0 win with success at Silverstone after inheriting the win, cliocup.fr, May 2019

“

No win is easy. My start was better than yesterday, but I couldn't really afford to cruise in the opening laps. I had a really good pace, which allowed me to pull away and go on for the win. It is good to be at the top of the general classification although it doesn't mean much after just four races. All I know for now is that I want more after these two victories!

”

Oscar makes it two Silverstone wins in two days, cliocup.fr, May 2019

“

I think it will take some time to completely sink in.

”

Oscar on securing the Formula Renault Eurocup at Yas Marina, thecheckeredflag.co.uk, November 2019

“My target is to move on to the FIA Formula 3 Championship, but nothing is done as yet as I need to look at my different options.”

Oscar on his next move, cliorally.com, October 2019

"With the world in lockdown and very strictly regulated international travel, possibly the most important moment of Piastri's career comes as he is granted exemption to travel from Australia to the United Kingdom and then serve a two-week quarantine once he arrives in the country. Piastri's exemption is also the firmest indication yet that FIA F3 will be racing."

Motorsport journalist Ida Wood gives a succinct summary of racing in the Covid-19 era, formulascout.com, May 2020

“I was pretty surprised to end up P2 in the practice session to be honest. I haven’t been here since 2018 and obviously none of us have driven the car for months, so it was a bit of a shock to the system getting back in. To be honest it’s still sinking in that we’ve actually just had qualifying because it’s all happened so fast. I’ll definitely take P3 and I can do some work with that tomorrow.”

Oscar gets back in the cockpit as the pandemic continues to rage, fiaformula3.com, July 2020

"I thought that my first Formula 3 race had ended in the first 10 seconds. I was hoping I didn't have much damage, which I didn't; it was pretty scary."

Oscar reflects on a belts-and-braces start to life in F3 having collided with Sebastian Fernandez at the race start, formulascout.com, July 2020

“Everything’s happening extremely fast at the moment. It feels very weird after four months of nothing to have already had a race. It’s a little bit odd, and having no fans is a bit strange. Getting out of the car and nobody being there was a little bit anticlimactic!”

Oscar starts F3 with a victory, but the behind-closed-doors race meant the win had a somewhat hollow feel, formulascout.com, July 2020

"

I haven't set myself any specific goals [for race two]. I obviously want to win, but we'll have to see what the race deals me.

"

Oscar on continuing his winning form, formulascout.com, July 2020

FACT

In a thrilling end to his first F3 season, Oscar Piastri went into the final race level on points, in joint first, with Logan Sergeant. Despite only finishing seventh, it was enough for Piastri to be crowned 2020 F3 champion.

"I think you're not human if you're not relieved when one of your championship rivals goes out. Obviously, I felt sorry for him, but if you say it doesn't provide a little bit of relief then you're lying."

An honest response from Oscar to title rival Logan Sergeant's early exit from the decisive final race of the season, nine.com.au, September 2020

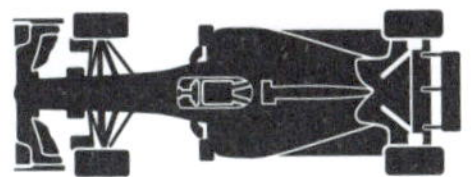

“I’d started to accept that wherever I ended up might not have been good enough to win the championship. I would have accepted it if that’s how it played out, but obviously it was a crazy weekend, so here I am, speaking to you as the champion.”

Oscar, still pinching himself after his F3 title, nine.com.au, September 2020

“

We’re speaking to a few teams at the moment for F2.

”

Oscar, trying to secure his future, nine.com.au, September 2020

"We've got some good options on the table. I'm expecting Mick [Schumacher] to move up to Formula One, which creates a free seat at Prema, but we haven't made any decisions yet, that will be our job for the next few weeks. Our relationship this year was really good, and if I do get the chance to stay at Prema next year I'd certainly be happy."

Oscar on playing musical chairs, nine.com.au, September 2020

CHAPTER FOUR

Oscar's Got Talent!

Oscar Piastri was fast becoming motorsport's hottest property – all he had to do now was move to the next level and prove he could realise his dream of becoming a Formula 1 driver...

“

I'm super excited to be racing with Prema in the 2021 FIA Formula 2 Championship.

”

Oscar secures his seat, formulascout.com, December 2020

“I'm very grateful to stay a part of the Prema family, and I'm looking forward to plenty more pizza and pasta!”

Oscar on the perks of the job, formulascout.com, December 2020

> "We are delighted to welcome Oscar to our FIA Formula 2 team."

Prema boss René Rosin welcomes his new recruit, formulascout.com, December 2020

“

Having witnessed his progress and success throughout the 2020 season, taking our relationship to the next step for the 2021 FIA Formula 2 Championship felt like the natural thing to do and we look forward to having him on track right from Bahrain.

”

More from René Rosin,
formulascout.com, December 2020

"

The second race [of the weekend] in Bahrain and it was a crazy one. We came out on top, so I want to give a massive thanks to PREMA. It was the right strategy call from the team to go onto softs.

"

Oscar on his maiden F2 win, fiaformula2.com, March 2021

“I am just riding the high at the minute, second race, first win. We struggled a bit at the beginning, but I couldn't be happier with the result and we will go again tomorrow.”

More on his maiden F2 win, fiaformula2.com, March 2021

"

We won the race, if you want to call it a race. The points are nice and I am glad that everybody is going to be okay, from the crash. That is the most important thing today and we will see you next week for the final round.

"

Piastri edges towards the F2 title after a scrappy victory in Jeddah, fiaformula2.com, December 2021

FACT

Oscar Piastri completed a historic hat-trick in Sprint Race 1 at Yas Marina, running a superb race from 10th to third to seal the Formula 2 crown with a podium – Oscar had now won the Formula 3, Formula Renault, and Formula 2 championships.

He is also only the third driver to win the F2 title in his rookie season, joining the esteemed company of Charles Leclerc and George Russell.

"The final race of F2 for the year is done and we managed to win the race, which is fantastic. It is a great way to end the year and a great way to end my junior career."

Oscar looks back on a successful year, grandprix.com.au, December 2021

“

Thank you everyone for your support and all of your messages after winning the championship. I have still got thousands unopened. It was very good to end the season on a high, I'll hopefully see you at some point on a grid in the future.

”

Oscar on the support he received, fiaformula2.com, December 2021

"[Piastri is] a great driver. The only problem he now has to deal with is [that] the expectation on him will be immense."

Former Red Bull boss Christian Horner foresees the pressures placed on such a talented young driver, formula1.com, September 2022

FACT

In 2021, Oscar Piastri became the first driver in history to win Formula Renault, Formula 3 and Formula 2 (or equivalent) championships in successive seasons.

An incredible feat.

FACT

Oscar Piastri completed his first test in a Formula 1 car at Bahrain's Sakhir International Circuit.

The 19-year-old was awarded the test in the Renault R.S.18 race car by the Renault DP World Formula 1 Team as recognition of his recent win in the FIA Formula 3 Championship.

"

That was pretty crazy – the Renault F1 car certainly lived up to the excitement. I was a little bit nervous beforehand, which is pretty normal, but after the first lap I got over that and focused on driving fast and having fun. I think I adapted quite well and got up to speed reasonably quickly.

"

Oscar on his first F1 test, oscarpiastri.com, October 2020

"

I really enjoyed the day, so a massive thank you to Renault for this opportunity. I'm feeling very lucky to drive an F1 car, not everyone gets to do it, so a massive thanks to them.

"

Oscar on the amazing opportunity, oscarpiastri.com, October 2020

“I’m super excited to be joining Alpine F1 Team as reserve driver.”

Oscar on his new role with Alpine, autosport.com, November 2021

"

I've proved myself in the junior formulas over the last couple of years and feel like I'm ready for Formula 1 now. Along with the trackside experience at race weekends, we will put together a substantial test programme in order to keep developing myself to grow even more prepared for a race seat.

I'm very thankful to Alpine for their support. We've enjoyed two very successful seasons together in the Academy and I'm grateful for the faith they've put in me for this next step with an eye on a bigger future.

”

Oscar on making the most of his reserve driver role, autosport.com, November 2021

"

I'm looking forward to being much more involved with the team and contributing to its intended success next season. The reserve driver role is the next step towards my aim for a race seat in 2023, which is very exciting.

"

Oscar on the chance to learn and contribute to the team's success, autosport.com, November 2021

“

At what was the start of the Oscar Piastri to McLaren story, the Australian is made available by Alpine to its rival team as reserve driver if his services are required. The agreement comes about after McLaren driver Daniel Ricciardo, a fellow Australian, goes down with COVID-19.

”

Journalist Ida Wood on the start of Oscar's journey to McLaren, formulascout.com, November 2022

CHAPTER FIVE

Moving Up a Gear

As his inevitable move to F1 moves along, there are still hurdles for Oscar Piastri to overcome...

“

It was not an easy journey to get to F1, especially for my mum. Seeing her firstborn go to the other side of the world at 14 didn’t come without its challenges. So it was a proud moment for her. There was some relief when I made it to F1 in the first place... that all the tough decisions and sacrifices for my family have paid off. And I get to live out my dreams.

”

Oscar on the relief of achieving his dream, GQ, August 2024

“

Alpine are putting together such an extensive test programme for this year and I think that speaks volumes about their belief in me.

”

Oscar on Alpine's investment, formula1.com, February 2022

“

I would have loved to have been straight into a race seat out of F2, but the way things have panned out, that hasn’t been possible… while I won’t be in a race seat, there is still a lot I can learn, experience the pretty hectic schedule of a F1 season and help out behind the scenes and fully focus on F1 – as that’s where I want to get to in the future.

”

Oscar looks on the bright side, formula1.com, February 2022

FACT

Oscar's restrictive role as reserve driver in 2022 meant no race action for the youngster – effectively a whole year out of racing and a definite bump in the road of his stellar rise to date.

“

It's been exciting and obviously something I've worked towards for a very, very long time. I think I started racing about 12 years ago now. It's been busy, but it's very cool to say I'm an F1 driver, that's for sure.

”

Oscar lets it all sink in, formula1.com, March 2023

“

Yeah, it was tough. Any racing driver wants to be racing as much as they can and being in that position, where the rules, because I won F2, said that I couldn't repeat F2, I quite literally had no more junior categories to race. That was a nice problem to have in one way. But still a problem, nonetheless.

”

Oscar reflecting on a frustrating 2022, formula1.com, February 2022

“I wanted to get to F1, of course, but I don’t know if I ever fully believed it was possible.”

Oscar on his early frustrations and hurdles to clear, thegentlemansjournal.com, 2024

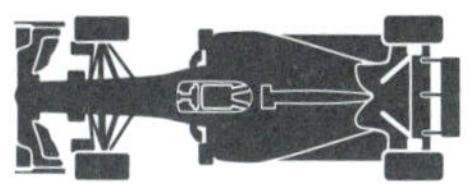

“I knew, even when I was karting and racing the cars in Formula 4, that the chances of reaching F1 are so slim, and I always tried to stay realistic. My main goal was to become a professional racing driver and be paid to drive race cars.”

The young Australian, keeping it real and making sure his feet were always grounded, thegentlemansjournal.com, 2024

“

Oscar is a bright and rare talent. We are proud to have nurtured and supported him through the difficult pathways of the junior formulae. Through our collaboration over the past four years, we have seen him develop and mature into a driver who is more than capable of taking the step up to Formula 1. As our reserve driver he has been exposed to the team at the track, factory and testing where

he has shown the maturity, promise and speed to ensure his promotion to our second seat alongside Esteban. Together, we believe the duo will give us the continuity we need to achieve our long-term goal of challenging for wins and championships.

”

Otmar Szafnauer, Alpine team principal, announces Piastri as Fernando Alonso's replacement, unbeknownst to Oscar Piastri, motorsport.com, August 2022

“

I understand that, without my agreement, Alpine F1 have put out a press release late this afternoon that I am driving for them next year. This is wrong and I have not signed a contract with Alpine for 2023. I will not be driving for Alpine next year.

”

Oscar takes to X (formerly Twitter) to rebuke Alpine's claims in his now-iconic response, just two hours after the press release announcement, August 2022

“The only contract to be recognised is the contact between McLaren and Piastri dated 4 July 2022. Piastri is entitled to drive for McLaren for the 2023 and 2024 seasons.”

Formula 1's Contract Recognition Board (CRB) issues a statement as Alpine lose their appeal to force Piastri to drive for them, bbc.co.uk, September 2022

“

It was in a service station car park in the UK. So, it wasn’t the most glamorous place to be signing an F1 contract, but it was a very, very special feeling.

”

Oscar recalls the unusual surroundings of a momentous moment in his F1 career, thegentlemansjournal.com, 2024

“Signing my F1 contract was a very special thing. Even if there was some controversy around it, it was very, very special.”

Oscar on that fateful moment, thegentlemansjournal.com, 2024

"

The team has a long tradition of giving young talent a chance, and I'm looking forward to working hard alongside Lando [Norris] to push the team towards the front of the grid. I'm focused on preparing for my F1 debut in 2023 and starting my F1 career in papaya.

"

Oscar's F1 career properly begins, bbc.co.uk, September 2022

“

I was going into a new category and it wasn’t just any category, it was F1.

”

Oscar on stepping into the biggest motorsport category in the world, manofmany.com, March 2024

“So it’s a bit different when you’ve got to remember 800 names compared to 30!”

Oscar on adjusting to the step-up into F1, formula1.com, March 2023

“He's going to have to get in and deliver against Lando, which is no mean feat. But you either sink or swim in this business. He's a very, very capable driver, [so] I'm sure he's going to do very well.”

Christian Horner on the challenges facing Oscar, racefans.net, September 2022

“

The first two races couldn’t have gone much worse I would say for the team.

”

Oscar on his opening two drives for McLaren, which saw him still pointless going into race three, therace.com, April 2023

"

[In] Bahrain we both had our issues, and Saudi with the contact wiping out both of us, so it was nice to be on the good end of other things going wrong for other people.

"

Oscar on securing his first points for McLaren in his home Australian Grand Prix, therace.com, April 2023

“

I’m definitely happy to have my first points on the board, especially here at home. Was a crazy race obviously, I think that’s the first race that I’ve had three red flags – probably most people’s first race like that. We kept ourselves out of trouble and ended up in the points at the end, which is great.

”

First points as an F1 driver in the bag at Oscar's home Grand Prix, foxsports.com.au, April 2023

FACT

Piastri became the first Formula 1 driver to finish on the podium in his rookie season since Lance Stroll in 2017, with a third place finish at the 2023 Japanese Grand Prix.

"It feels very special, definitely. I'll remember it for a very, very long time."

Oscar on his first podium in Japan, drive.com, September 2023

"I can't thank the team enough for giving me this opportunity. There's not many people in the world that get this opportunity in their whole life and I've managed to have it in my first season."

More of Oscar's reaction to his first podium in Japan, drive.com, September 2023

"The safety cars were my friend today, definitely, once Max got behind me."

More on his first podium in Japan, drive.com, September 2023

“

A first sprint win sounds pretty cool.

”

Oscar on his maiden sprint win in Qatar, bbc.co.uk, October 2023

FACT

In his maiden F1 season. Oscar Piastri finished ninth in the World Drivers' Championship with two podiums and 97 points, 108 behind teammate Lando Norris in sixth.

Despite some struggles, his results still led to a multi-year contract extension with McLaren until at least the end of 2026.

> “Keeping Oscar was an easy decision for the team to make.”

McLaren team principal Andrea Stella comments on Piastri's contract extension, bbc.co.uk, September 2023

“I want to be fighting it out at the front of the grid with this team and I am excited by the vision and foundations that are already being laid to get us there.”

Oscar on extending his McLaren contract, bbc.co.uk, September 2023

"The welcome that I have received and the relationships that I have built make this feel like home already. The team's consistent commitment to me has made me feel incredibly valued and the desire from the team for me to be part of its long-term future made this an easy decision."

More from Oscar, bbc.co.uk, September 2023

“

It’s very, very special. This is really the day I dreamed of as a kid, standing on the top step of an F1 podium.

”

Oscar, after securing his first ever F1 victory in Hungary, cnn.com, July 2024

"

[It was] obviously a bit complicated at the end, but I put myself in the right position at the start, and thank you to the team for an amazing effort and amazing car.

"

Oscar on that first F1 triumph, and a reference to the controversy surrounding team orders, cnn.com, July 2024

"It's tough, but I know what Oscar's done for me in the past. I think this is a little bit different but, yeah, at the same time, I got told to let him past and I did. It's always tough when you're fighting for a win, and a win means so much to me and also to him."

McLaren teammate Lando Norris followed team orders and allowed Piastri to pass to secure his first win, cnn.com, July 2024

FACT

Oscar Piastri became the fifth Australian to win a world championship grand prix, following in the footsteps of Jack Brabham, Alan Jones, Mark Webber and Daniel Ricciardo.

Piastri also became the first F1 race winner born in the 21st century.

“That was probably the most stressful afternoon of my life!”

Oscar on his second F1 win with a stunning drive at the Azerbaijan Grand Prix, autosport.com, September 2024

“

I was very happy with this afternoon, that definitely goes down as one of the best races of my career I think. After the first stint I thought we'd be second at absolute best, but we managed to gain time after the pit stop. I knew when I was in DRS on that one lap I knew I had to try everything to make it stick because if I didn't I definitely wouldn't win the race.

”

More on his success at Azerbaijan, autosport.com, September 2024

FACT

Oscar Piastri ended the 2024 season fourth in the World Drivers' Championship on 292 points – 82 behind teammate and runner-up Lando Norris.

He recorded two victories and eight podiums, helping McLaren win their first World Constructors' Championship since 1998.

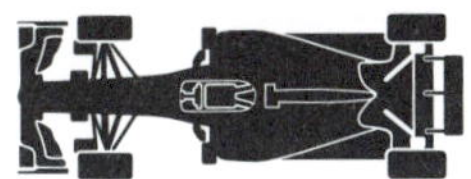

"It's a great feeling knowing that I'm part of McLaren's long-term vision. The team had the belief in me when we signed in 2022, and the journey we've gone on over the past two seasons to help return McLaren to the very top of the sport has been incredible."

On signing a new multi-year deal with McLaren, formula1.com, March 2025

CHAPTER SIX

Race to the Finish

With a new deal and a rivalry with teammate Lando Norris that could prove a tinderbox in years to come, the sky is the limit for Oscar Piastri...

“

He’s definitely a tough teammate to go up against, but I think that’s a good thing. You want to always compare yourself to the best.

”

Oscar on Lando Norris,
thegentlemansjournal.com, 2024

“

You can’t just beat them once and say, ‘That was good, I beat a World Champion.’ You have to do that consistently and treat them as any other driver.

”

Oscar has always set the bar high,
mclaren.com, *March 2025*

“

You have to forget about the names, the history, the achievements. It’s just another person you’re trying to beat. They’re still human.

”

Oscar on going up against the best, mclaren.com, March 2025

“

I’m going in with the hope and ambition to fight for the Drivers’ title and to help the team retain the Constructors’ title. With the season we’ve just had, it would be silly to aim for anything less – certainly to prepare for anything less – but we’ll see how we come out of the gates and reassess from there.

”

Oscar on his goals for the 2025 season, mclaren.com, March 2025

“

It is always a nice confidence booster when you come out on top, because you are racing against the best of the best, but you can’t get caught up in it.

”

Oscar on what motivates him, mclaren.com, March 2025

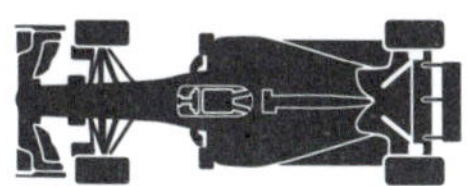

"

We're a team of over 1,000 people, and I'm just one of the two guys that gets to drive the car.

"

Piastri boils down his job, GQ, August 2024

"Yeah, it's cool, I mean that's where I made my social media name for myself on Twitter a few years ago, and now my mum's doing the same, mainly by making fun of me, but that's okay, she's my mum, she's allowed to!"

Oscar on his mum's social media cult following, planetf1.com, November 2023

“

It’s just the risk, and it’s not so much Oscar, it’s people around him. He’s very cautious by nature, and he’s very calculated and clever in the way that he does everything. He took on Max at the first corner, which was a bit horrifying. But typically, he won’t take risks. But you can’t trust that those around him won’t.

”

Nicole Piastri on being a nervous parent watching her son’s races, gpfans.com, April 2025

"When we went to Silverstone, both (Lando and I) had the upgrades, qualified second and third and finished second and fourth, I think everyone kind of went, 'Okay, that was not a fluke.'"

Oscar on McLaren's form, manofmany.com, March 2024

"There is also a growing onus on athletes to be able to speak about more than just what they do on the track. I'm still finding my feet with what exactly does add meaning for me but this is a start."

Oscar on the pressures of the job beyond racing, GQ, August 2024

“

Oscar through his junior categories has been exceptional... So I think last year entering Formula 1 for him was... it's a big step. But time and time again, he has shown that he's ready to race at the front against the big guys. And he's fine for that. Respectful, hard, clean.

”

Oscar's mentor and manager, Mark Webber, sings his praises and offers sound advice, thesportsrush.com, September 2024

"There's definitely still things I need to work on. I'm [slowly] getting everything right and to a level that I'm happy with."

Oscar on his steady progression in F1, therace.com, August 2023

"

Relaxed intensity is a trait Piastri shares with Max Verstappen, although where they differ is that Piastri – so far – has not exhibited any kind of outburst inside the car. Now, that might change (it surely will) when he finds himself in more high-stakes scenarios. But McLaren's not observed any indication that Piastri can be knocked off his stride that easily.

"

The Race journalist Scott Mitchell-Malm's portrait of Piastri, therace.com, August 2023

“

It kind of makes sense – if you think, what would the personality of a Formula 1 driver be if you’d never met any? But I’m not sure I’ve met that many who I would describe as calm and intense.

”

McLaren race engineer Tom Stallard on Piastri’s unique qualities, therace.com, August 2023

“Stress isn’t an emotion one would associate with Piastri. His calm, collected demeanor has been present right from his junior days. The demands of fighting at the front in F1 haven’t changed him one bit.”

The New York Times *journalist Luke Smith looks deeper into Piastri's psyche,* The New York Times, September 2024

"

That was, I think, one of the best drives I've ever seen him pull off. Obviously under a lot of pressure, defensive, very decisive in the move itself. And up against a world-class driver – Charles [Leclerc] around here is absolutely magical. So to beat him is a pretty big deal.

"

Mark Webber on Piastri's epic win at Baku,
The New York Times, September 2024

"

Describe myself in three words... I would say relaxed, calculating and chilled!

"

Oscar's response is accurate, formula1.com, June 2024

“

It’s the word ‘innit’. Just tagging it on to the end of everything. For me, that was very alien when I first came to the UK. It still is very alien. Admittedly, I feel like it’s a certain... demographic that probably use that a lot. It's not part of my vocabulary but it was certainly an eye-opening experience amongst a lot of other slang.

”

Oscar on his favorite British slang, imdb.com

"

From the outside, it's as if his pulse is a flat line at all times, and I can think of few drivers who could or can control their emotions and mind like that. Alain Prost, 'the professor', would be one.

"

Former F1 driver and legendary pundit Martin Brundle shares his admiration for Piastri, skysports.com, April 2025

“

He’s very consistent. He doesn’t show his emotions, and he doesn’t go up and down that much.

”

Former F3 teammate Frederik Vesti on Piastri's calm demeanor, f1oversteer.com, July 2025

“

He’s very solid. He’s very calm in his approach, and I like that. It shows on track. He delivers when he has to, barely makes mistakes – and that’s what you need when you want to fight for a championship.

”

Multiple world champion Max Verstappen’s praise for his title rival, bbc.co.uk, April 2025

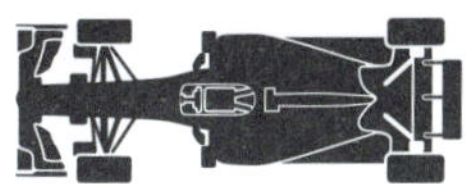

"With Mark by his side, he's helping him a lot. It's great. People learn from their own careers. That's what I had with my dad, and Mark is advising Oscar. At the end of the day, Oscar is using his talent, and that's great to see."

Verstappen on Mark Webber's influence on Oscar, bbc.co.uk, April 2025

“

My great great grandfather was Chinese so I think that makes this my 1/16 home race?

”

Oscar Piastri on X, in his ongoing quest to make every race a home race, April 2024

“Good time to mention that I'm also 3/16 Italian?”

More from Oscar's quest, X, May 2024

“

I found a lot of pace in Q3. Q1 and Q2 I was genuinely struggling and the car came alive, I came alive in Q3. The laps were a little bit scruffy but I'm just pumped to be on pole.

”

Oscar claims his maiden pole position at the 2025 Chinese Grand Prix, skysports.com, March 2025

“

It’s been an incredible weekend from start to finish – the car’s been pretty mega the whole time.

”

Piastri converts a maiden pole position to victory at the 2025 Chinese Grand Prix, formula1.com, March 2025

“

Once you’re done playing games on your phone, Osc, do you think you could FaceTime me so I can congratulate you on your win in China?

”

Oscar’s mum sends him a message via Instagram after seeing a picture of her son playing games following his win in China, thesportsrush.com, March 2023

"I'm very proud to do it here in Bahrain as well; it's obviously a very important race for us given our owners. It's never been a track that's been kind to us, so it's nice to finally have that first win for the team here."

Oscar claims a fourth F1 Grand Prix victory in Bahrain, formula1.com, April 2025

“

Nice work today, Osc. Does this mean I can get rid of some of these finally?

”

Nicole Piastri posts on X next to pictures of his karting trophies back home, suggesting she create more space for his growing F1 collection, essentiallysports.com, October 2023

“

I’m sure there’s going to be a hell of a party! I’m not going to get involved, because I’ve got to race again next week...

”

Oscar after the Bahrain Grand Prix, formula1.com, April 2025

“

Great race. We did the parts we needed to right. Still need a bit more I think, Max was a little bit too close for our liking but a great race and a great weekend.

”

Oscar follows up his win in Bahrain by winning the 2025 Saudi Arabia Grand Prix and also becoming the first Australian since 2010 to lead the World Championship, formula1.com, April 2025

"I remember two years ago in Miami we were genuinely the slowest team. To now have won the grand prix by over 35 seconds to third is an unbelievable result."

Oscar on the strong start to the 2025 season,
The Guardian, *March 2025*

“

Hard to complain; it has been a great year and this weekend has been exactly the kind of weekend I was looking for. We executed everything we needed to when it counted and that's all we could ask for.

”

On winning the 2025 Spanish Grand Prix,
bbc.co.uk, June 2025

“

The team gave me a great car once again. It’s a lot of fun winning races at the moment and I’ve been enjoying it and I hope the team are too.

”

More from Oscar on his win in Spain, bbc.co.uk, June 2025

"

If you're giving Edie the champagne, you're looking after her tonight, right, Osc?

"

Oscar's mum takes to X to make sure he looks after his sister Edie given his champagne comment, June 2025

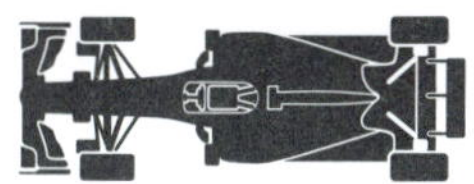

“

Pretty sure I would’ve remembered that!

”

Oscar’s mum – at it again! She reacts on X to a fan putting a comment of a picture featuring Oscar with Fernando Alonso saying, "The goat father and the goat son", November 2023

"Behind the scenes, he makes sure that my contracts turn out as they should. It's about details you don't even think about yourself."

Oscar on manager Mark Webber's mentorship role, thesportsrush.com, March 2025

"

Alpine still managed to find a way to f*** me up all these years later, huh?

"

Piastri shows his frustration after Alpine drivers impede him at various stages of the 2025 Austrian Grand Prix, autosport.com, June 2025

“

I think that’s, as a Formula 1 driver, a big component of your profession, so it’s something that’s not lost on him, that over your journey, when you’re up against Max, Charles [Leclerc], Lando, Lewis [Hamilton], like these guys in the first few years, there’s some serious artillery there over one lap.

”

Piastri’s manager and former F1 star Webber comments on Oscar’s improved driving over one lap, formula1.com, April 2025

“As I say to him, you have the most experience the day you retire, so keep learning.”

Mark Webber on Oscar's continued education, formula1.com, April 2025

“

I just try to keep it normal. I get to do an amazing job that I'm very lucky to do, and I say job very loosely because it's certainly not a real job. To be able to do that is already an incredible place to be.

”

Oscar on his incredible job, manofmany.com, March 2024

“

For me, I just want to try and leave each weekend feeling like I've done a good job and being satisfied with my performance regardless of where I end up. Definitely with how we've finished the season, it's hard to not be excited for what could come. So let's see what we've got.

”

Oscar on what constitutes a job well done, manofmany.com, March 2024

“

It is difficult to have true friends on the grid, because at the end of the day, you’re trying to beat them all the time.

”

Oscar on the challenges of F1 friendships, planetf1.com, December 2024

"

Obviously, Lando and I are teammates, and we get along well. We work very well together, but, of course, we each want to outdo the other. That's just the nature of racing drivers. But we do get along well.

"

Oscar on his teammate, rival and friend (for now!), Lando Norris, speedcafe.com, August 2024

“If we’re fighting for first and second every weekend, then there’s always a little bit more tension, I guess.”

Oscar’s honest appraisal of his relationship with Lando Norris, thegentlemansjournal.com, 2024

"We've seen in the past, look at Lewis [Hamilton] and Nico [Rosberg], when you're fighting for first and second, that's when things can sometimes change a little bit. We've been in a position like that a few times now."

More on the rivalry with Lando, planetf1.com, December 2024

“

I’m not going to say much, I’ll get myself in trouble. Well done to Nico, I think that’s the highlight of the day. I’ll leave it there.

”

Oscar on the 10-second penalty imposed at the 2025 British Grand Prix, with a word of congratulations to Nico Hulkenberg, who ended his long wait for a podium finish, formula1.com, July 2025.

"Apparently you can't brake behind the safety car anymore. I did it for five laps before that. Thanks to the crowd for a great event, thanks for sticking through the weather. I still like Silverstone, even if I don't like it today."

More thoughts on the 10-second penalty, formula1.com, July 2025

“

We jokingly said last year that we want to give McLaren a problem having to build new trophy cabinets. If we keep going the way we are, that might actually be a problem.

”

Oscar on a nice problem to have, GQ, August 2024

“Longer term, I want to win World Championships. That’s what we’re all here for, right?”

Oscar's goals are clear, planetf1.com, December 2024

“

When the pressure isn’t on, it’s easy to look great, but when the pressure is really on, and the consequences are much bigger, that is when you see the cream rise to the top.

”

Oscar on dealing with pressure, mclaren.com, March 2025